Mar 2016

THE AFRICAN AMERICAN
EXPERIENCE
FROM SLAVERY TO THE PRESIDENCY

THE RISE OF THE
JIM CROW ERA

EDITED BY
MARIA HUSSEY

Britannica®
Educational Publishing

IN ASSOCIATION WITH

ROSEN
EDUCATIONAL SERVICES

Published in 2016 by Britannica Educational Publishing (a trademark of Encyclopædia Britannica, Inc.) in association with The Rosen Publishing Group, Inc.
29 East 21st Street, New York, NY 10010

Distributed exclusively by Rosen Publishing.
To see additional Britannica Educational Publishing titles, go to rosenpublishing.com.

First Edition

Britannica Educational Publishing
J.E. Luebering: Director, Core Reference Group
Anthony L. Green: Editor, Compton's by Britannica

Rosen Publishing
Hope Lourie Killcoyne: Executive Editor
Amelie von Zumbusch: Editor
Nelson Sá: Art Director
Brian Garvey: Designer
Cindy Reiman: Photography Manager

Library of Congress Cataloging-in-Publication Data

The rise of the Jim Crow era/edited by Maria Hussey.—First edition.
      pages cm.—(The African American experience: from slavery to the presidency)
Includes bibliographical references and index.
ISBN 978-1-68048-042-9 (library bound)
1. African Americans—Civil rights—Southern States—History—19th century—Juvenile literature.
2. African Americans—Segregation--Southern States—History—19th century—Juvenile literature.
3. African Americans—Legal status, laws, etc.—Southern States—History. 4. Southern States—Race relations—Juvenile literature. 5. Racism—Southern States—History—Juvenile literature. 6. African Americans—History—1863-1877—Juvenile literature. 7. African Americans—History—1877-1964—Juvenile literature. I. Hussey, Maria.
E185.92.R58 2015
323.1196'073075—dc23

2014039059

Manufactured in the United States of America

Photo credits: Cover (W.E.B. Dubois), pp. 5, 9, 13, 17, 26, 29, 30, 33, 38, 44, 46, 49 Library of Congress, Washington, D.C.; cover (background) CBS Photo Archive/Getty Images; p. 11 © Collection of the New-York Historical Society, USA/Bridgeman Images; p. 14 Bibliotheque des Arts Decoratifs, Paris, France/Archives Charmet/Bridgeman Images; p. 19 Encyclopædia Britannica, Inc.; pp. 20-21 © Newagen Archive/The Image Works; p. 24 Jose Gil/Shutterstock.com; p. 34 Johnston (Frances Benjamin) Collection/Library of Congress, Washington D.C. (LC-J601-302); p. 35 National Archives and Records Administration/U.S. Department of Agriculture, CC BY 2.0; p. 41 Apic/Hulton Archive/Getty Images; p. 42 © TopFoto/The Image Works; p. 50 John Deakin/Picture Post/Getty Images; pp. 52 Joe Amon/The Denver Post/Getty Images; p. 54 R. Gates/Hulton Archive/Getty Images; p. 56 Schomburg Center, NYPL/Art Resource, NY; p. 60 J. T. Vintage/Bridgeman Images; pp. 62-63 Afro Newspaper/Gado/Archive Photos/Getty Images; interior pages background texture © iStockphoto.com/Piotr Krześlak.

CONTENTS

J im Crow laws were designed to create two separate societies in the South—one white, the other black. Separate areas in which to live, separate railroad cars, drinking fountains, hospitals, restaurants, schools, even separate cemeteries—separate but equal in theory but certainly not in practice.

These laws existed to enforce racial segregation in the South from about 1877, which marked the end of the formal Reconstruction period, to the beginning of the civil rights movement in the 1950s. *Jim Crow* was the name of a minstrel routine (actually *Jump Jim Crow*) performed beginning in 1828 by its author, Thomas Dartmouth Rice, and by many imitators. The term came to be a derogatory epithet for blacks and a designation for their segregated life.

From the late 1870s, Southern state legislatures passed laws requiring the separation of whites from "persons of color" in public transportation and schools. Anyone known or strongly suspected to be of some degree of

This sign from a bus station in Rome, Georgia, points to the location of the station's "colored," or African American, waiting room.

black ancestry was for this purpose a "person of color." The pre–Civil War distinction favoring those whose ancestry was known to be mixed—particularly the half-French "free persons of color" in Louisiana—was abandoned. The segregation principle was extended to parks, cemeteries, theaters, and restaurants in an effort to prevent any contact between blacks and whites as equals. It was codified on local and state levels and most famously with the "separate but equal" decision of the U.S. Supreme Court in *Plessy v. Ferguson* (1896).

During this period, a number of leaders emerged to fight for the African Americans oppressed by these unfair laws. Booker T. Washington, the dominant African American leader at the turn of the 20th century, called on blacks to cease agitating for political and social rights and to concentrate instead on working to improve their economic conditions. Meanwhile, black leaders opposed to Washington began to emerge. The historian and sociologist W.E.B. Du Bois criticized Washington's accommodationist philosophy in *The Souls of Black Folk* (1903). Others were William Monroe Trotter, the militant editor of the *Boston Guardian*, and Ida B. Wells-Barnett, a journalist and a crusader against lynching. They insisted that blacks should demand their full civil rights and that a liberal education was necessary for the development of black leadership. At a meeting in Niagara Falls, Ontario, in 1905, Du Bois and other black leaders who shared his views founded the Niagara Movement. Members of the Niagara group joined with concerned liberal and radical whites to organize the National Association for the Advancement of Colored People (NAACP; initially known as the National Negro Committee) in 1909. The NAACP journal *The Crisis*, edited by Du Bois, became an effective organ of propaganda for black rights. The NAACP won its first major legal case in 1915, when the U.S. Supreme Court outlawed the "grandfather clause," a constitutional device used in the South to disenfranchise blacks.

CHAPTER ONE

THE REBIRTH OF WHITE SUPREMACY

The years immediately following the Civil War brought both challenges and new opportunities for African Americans. Many newly freed slaves had trouble finding work and struggled to feed, clothe, and house themselves and their families. Given a free hand in managing their own affairs, the Southern states enacted a number of laws intended to assure that white supremacy would continue. These laws are known as the black codes. In many ways they resembled the slave codes that had existed before emancipation. The black codes intended to secure a steady supply of cheap labor and continued to assume the inferiority of the freed slaves. These laws permitted blacks to legally marry other blacks but did not allow them to vote or to serve on juries. Blacks could testify in court only in cases involving members of their own race. Provisions of the codes compelled blacks to work, no matter what the terms or the conditions under which they worked. The areas in which the freed slaves could purchase or rent property were specified. Punishments were imposed on blacks who owned firearms, who were absent from work, or who were "insulting" to white people.

RADICAL RECONSTRUCTION

However, the Radical Republicans, a group in the U.S. Congress, were upset that the people who had controlled the Confederacy were still in power in the

While freedmen were no longer trapped in slavery, most of their lives remained difficult. This group of freedmen was photographed in Richmond, Virginia.

THE RACIST ROOTS OF "JIM CROW"

Even the name "Jim Crow" is an example of white supremacy. "Jim Crow" was a character created by Thomas Dartmouth Rice (also known as Jim Crow Rice and Daddy Rice), who is regarded as the father of the minstrel show. Rice was an itinerant actor when his song and dance *Jump Jim Crow*, first presented in Louisville in 1828, caught the public fancy and made him one of the most popular specialty performers of his day. Although he was not the first white entertainer to perform in blackface, Rice created a vogue for impersonating African Americans in both the United States and England through a series of extremely successful tours. He wrote and appeared in *Ginger Blue*, *Jim Crow in London*, and a burlesque of *Othello*. These engendered the stereotypes for the skits in the popular minstrel shows that evolved in the 1840s, primarily as a result of Rice's success.

Blackface minstrelsy, also called blackface, is an indigenous American theatrical form that constituted a subgenre of the minstrel show. Intended as comic entertainment, blackface minstrelsy was performed by a group of white minstrels (traveling musicians) with black-painted faces, whose material caricatured the singing and dancing of slaves. The form reached the pinnacle of its popularity between 1850 and 1870, when it enjoyed sizeable audiences in both the United States and Britain.

By 1846 its unique three-part structure had formed: a repartee between the master of ceremonies, or interlocutor,

This hand-colored engraving from the 1830s shows Thomas Dartmouth Rice performing his Jim Crow routine.

and the end men (Brudder Tambo and Brudder Bones); followed by the "olio," or variety section; and ending with a one-act skit. Claiming to use credible black humor and traits, the minstrel show reached its peak between 1850 and 1870. Although it offered lively entertainment, it perpetuated negative stereotypes of blacks that lasted long after the shows had vanished.

South. They called for new governments to be set up. They expanded the Freedmen's Bureau, which provided food and medical care for former slaves, as well as set up schools for them. Congress passed the Civil Rights Act of 1866, which defined all persons born in the United States as national citizens, who were to enjoy equality before the law. White Southerners who had participated in the rebellion were disenfranchised (barred from voting). Blacks, white Southerners who had not joined the rebellion, and white Northerners who moved to the South were allowed to vote and assumed political leadership in the Southern states.

From the outset of Radical Reconstruction, the Ku Klux Klan and other terrorist organizations sought to convert the biracial governments of the South into governments of white men only. These organizations included the Red Shirts, the Regulators, the White Line, and the Knights of the White Camelia. They directed their principal efforts at preventing blacks from voting. The terrorist groups maimed, whipped, and hanged blacks and their white allies and drove them out of the communities in which they lived. Some of the most respected white Southerners were silently sympathetic to the use of such methods to overthrow the Reconstruction governments. The few soldiers in the region, including those in state militias, were no match for a militant, armed white South.

THE KU KLUX KLAN

A secret U.S. terrorist organization, the Ku Klux Klan led underground resistance against the civil rights and political power of newly freed black slaves during

This depiction of one of the secret societies that terrorized African Americans during Reconstruction shows members in robes resembling those famously worn by the Ku Klux Klan.

the Reconstruction period. The Klan's goal was to reestablish the dominance of the prewar plantation aristocracy. It was revived in an altered form in the 20th century.

Organized in 1866 by Confederate veterans as a social club in Pulaski, Tennessee, the Ku Klux Klan was

This 1872 engraving from the magazine *Harper's Weekly* shows Ku Klux Klan members who were arrested for attempted murder in Tishomingo County, Mississippi.

restructured along political and racial lines a year later in Nashville, Tennessee. Sometimes called the Invisible Empire of the South, the KKK, or the Klan, it was presided over by a grand wizard and a descending hierarchy of grand dragons, grand titans, and grand cyclopses. They took the name of the organization from the Greek word *kyklos*, meaning "circle," and the English word "clan." Dressed in robes and hoods designed to frighten victims and to prevent identification by federal troops, Klansmen whipped and killed freed slaves in nighttime raids. With intimidation and threats, Klansmen drove blacks and their white sympathizers out of their communities, destroying their crops and burning their houses and barns.

Because of an increase in the number of kidnappings and murders, the grand wizard of the Klan ordered it disbanded in 1869, but local groups remained active. The rest of the country reacted strongly to the increased violence in the South, and Congress passed the Force Act in 1870 and the Ku Klux Klan Act in 1871, authorizing the president to suspend the writ of habeas corpus, suppress disturbances by force, and impose heavy penalties on terrorist organizations. Resulting federal prosecution of Klan members, however, created widespread Southern sympathy in their behalf. As Southern political power gradually reverted to traditional white Democratic control during the 1870s, the need for anti-Republican, antiblack organizations to remain secret decreased.

CHAPTER TWO

POLITICAL, ECONOMIC, AND SOCIAL DISPARITY

The rebirth of white supremacy in the South was accompanied by the growth of enforced racial separation. Starting with Tennessee in 1870, all the Southern states reenacted laws prohibiting racial intermarriage. They also passed Jim Crow laws segregating blacks and whites in almost all public places. By 1885 most Southern states had officially segregated their public schools.

The Jim Crow laws were part of an effort by white Americans to ensure that African Americans had and

The Constitution granted African American men the right to vote in 1870. This print by A. R. Waud shows a group of black men lined up to vote for the first time.

continued to have less power than white Americans. This applied to economic and social power as well as political power and left African Americans at a real disadvantage on several fronts.

POLITICAL LIMITATIONS

Under Radical Reconstruction, African Americans in the South gained real political power for the first time. However black political power was short-lived. Northern politicians grew increasingly conciliatory to the white South, so that by 1872 virtually all leaders of the Confederacy had been pardoned and were able to vote and hold office. By means of economic pressure and the terrorist activities of violent antiblack groups, such as the Ku Klux Klan, most blacks were kept away from the polls. By 1877, with the withdrawal of the last federal troops from the South, Southern whites were again in full control. Blacks were disenfranchised by the provisions of new state constitutions such as those adopted by Mississippi in 1890 and by South Carolina and Louisiana in 1895. Only a few Southern black elected officials lingered on. No black was to serve in the U.S. Congress for three decades after the departure of George H. White of North Carolina in 1901.

Many states passed grandfather clauses as a way to keep African Americans from being able to vote at all. A grandfather clause is a provision that was formerly included in constitutions of several U.S. Southern states that excused from other suffrage tests those who have served in any war and their descendants and those who were voters before Jan. 1, 1867, and their descendants. Grandfather clauses were

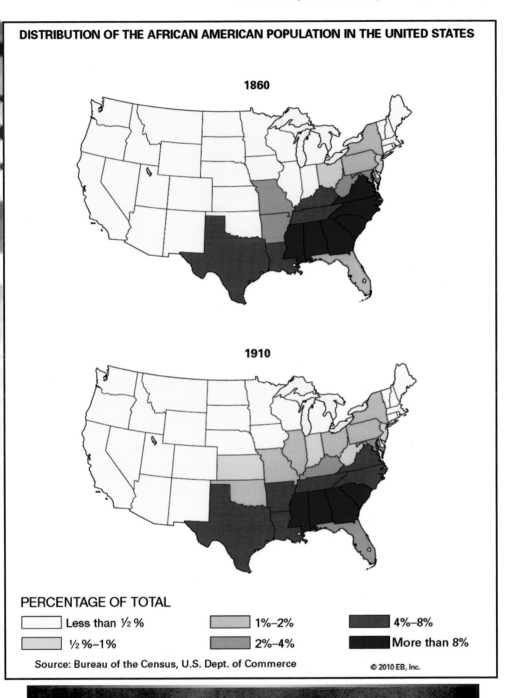

DISTRIBUTION OF THE AFRICAN AMERICAN POPULATION IN THE UNITED STATES

1860

1910

PERCENTAGE OF TOTAL

Less than ½%   1%–2%   4%–8%

½%–1%   2%–4%   More than 8%

Source: Bureau of the Census, U.S. Dept. of Commerce

© 2010 EB, Inc.

Most of the African American population remained in the South in the half-century following the Civil War, as you can see in these maps.

MOVING TO FIND WORK

In search of improvement, many blacks migrated westward. Some freed slaves went to Texas, which offered higher wages for agricultural work. Others went to Indian Territory (now Oklahoma) or Kansas to seek land to farm. In Kansas and later Oklahoma territory, blacks as well as whites could become homesteaders, pioneers who received essentially free land from the government if they settled it and cultivated it for a set period. Many blacks believed that Kansas, which had been the site of much antislavery activity, would provide the greatest opportunities for political, social, and economic equality. Some black men, known as buffalo soldiers, joined the U.S. Army, fighting Indians on the frontier.

adopted as means of restricting suffrage to white voters. In 1915 the Supreme Court declared the grandfather clause unconstitutional because it violated equal voting rights guaranteed by the Fifteenth Amendment.

ECONOMIC DISADVANTAGES

For the most part, the freed black slaves were without financial resources. Their hopes for a

Landlords not only took part—often 30 percent to 50 percent—of sharecroppers' crops, but also charged high rates for seeds, tools, and the use of farm animals.

redistribution of the large Southern estates were not realized. The only option for most of the former slaves was to resume work on the plantations owned by whites. Some of the former slaves worked for wages, but many were compelled to become sharecroppers. The black sharecroppers worked the farmland owned by whites; the sharecroppers were not paid wages for their work, but they did not give the landowners money for rent. Instead, at the end of the year, the sharecroppers kept part of the crop and gave the rest to the landowners. The very low incomes provided by the grueling sharecropping system forced on blacks a miserable existence that was little better than slavery.

Blacks received only a small share of the increasing number of industrial jobs in Southern cities. And relatively few rural blacks in the South owned their own farms, most remaining poor sharecroppers heavily in debt to white landlords. The largely urban Northern blacks fared little better. The jobs they sought were given to white European immigrants.

"SEPARATE BUT EQUAL"

Plessy v. Ferguson was a U.S. Supreme Court case concerning whether racial segregation laws requiring African Americans and whites to use different public facilities were constitutional. The case was decided on May 18, 1896. The court's decision in the case established the controversial doctrine of "separate but equal." According to this doctrine, laws that required African Americans and whites to use separate public facilities were constitutional as long as the facilities were reasonably equal. (In fact, public facilities for African Americans were inferior to those intended for whites.) The *Plessy v. Ferguson* decision served as a controlling judicial precedent for more than fifty years.

THE CASE

Plessy v. Ferguson originated in 1892 as a challenge to Louisiana's Separate Car Act. This law required that all railroads operating in the state provide "equal but separate accommodations" for white and African American passengers. Passengers were only allowed in the rail cars assigned to their race. To challenge the constitutionality of the law, a group of citizens in New Orleans formed a committee to generate a test case. They had Homer Plessy, who was seven-eighths white and one-eighth African American, purchase a rail ticket and sit in a rail car reserved for white passengers. After Plessy refused to move to a car for African Americans, he was arrested. He was tried and found guilty in U.S. District Court, and a state supreme court upheld the verdict. The case was then taken to the U.S. Supreme Court.

Plessy argued that the Separate Car Act was unconstitutional. He contended that it violated both the Thirteenth Amendment, which prohibited slavery, and the Fourteenth Amendment, which granted full and equal rights of citizenship to African Americans.

THE COURT RULES

Rejecting these arguments, the Supreme Court ruled 7 to 1 against Plessy (one justice did not participate). Associate Justice Henry Billings Brown wrote the majority opinion—which did not actually contain the phrase "separate but equal." He held that the Separate Car Act did not conflict with the Thirteenth Amendment because it did not reestablish slavery or constitute a "badge" of

HOMER ADOLPH PLESSY
1862-1925

ON JUNE 7, 1892, HOMER ADOLPH PLESSY DEFIED A LOUISIANA LAW THAT SEGREGATED RAILROAD TRAINS ON THE BASIS OF RACE. HE WAS ARRESTED AND BECAME THE DEFENDANT IN THE MAY 18, 1896 UNITED STATES SUPREME COURT DECISION OF PLESSY V. FERGUSON, WHICH CONDONED "SEPARATE BUT EQUAL" FACILITIES IN THE UNITED STATES. SPONSORED BY A NEW ORLEANS GROUP, CALLED THE *COMITÉ DES CITOYENS*," PLESSY'S CIVIL DISOBEDIENCE MARKED ONE OF THE FIRST LEGAL CHALLENGES TO THE SEPARATION OF RACES IN THE SOUTH FOLLOWING THE RECONSTRUCTION PERIOD. THOUGH HE LOST THE CASE IN 1896, THE COURT LATER UPHELD PLESSY'S FOURTEENTH AMENDMENT ARGUMENTS IN 1954 IN BROWN V. BOARD OF EDUCATION. THE COMITÉ DES CITOYENS INCLUDED LOUIS ANDRE MARTINET, ATTORNEY AND PUBLISHER OF *THE CRUSADER* NEWSPAPER, AND RODOLPHE DESDUNES, A WRITER FOR *THE CRUSADER*, WHO IS ENTOMBED IN ST. LOUIS CEMETERY NO. II. LEAD ATTORNEYS IN THE CASE WERE JAMES WALKER OF NEW ORLEANS AND THE NOTED RECONSTRUCTION AUTHOR, ALBION W. TOURGÉE OF NEW YORK.

This plaque hangs on Plessy's tomb. As someone with both African and French ancestors, Plessy had been considered a Creole by pre–Jim Crow racial classifications.

slavery or servitude. Brown further concluded that the act did not conflict with the Fourteenth Amendment. That amendment, he argued, was intended to secure only the legal equality of African Americans and whites, not their social equality. Brown concluded that the racial segregation of rail passengers did not by itself imply the legal inferiority of either race. "If one race be inferior to the other socially," he wrote, "the Constitution of the United States cannot put them upon the same plane."

The lone judge who ruled for Plessy was Associate Justice John Marshall Harlan. Harlan is considered to be one of the most forceful dissenters in the history of the court. His best known dissents favored the rights of African Americans as guaranteed, in his view, by constitutional amendments.

In his dissenting opinion, he argued that the Separate Car Act was universally understood to assume the inferiority of African Americans. As such, it imposed a badge of servitude upon them in violation of the Thirteenth Amendment. The effect of the act, he argued, was to interfere with the personal liberty and freedom of movement of both African Americans and whites. It thus conflicted with the principle of legal equality in the Fourteenth Amendment. Harlan wrote:

Our Constitution is color-blind and neither knows nor tolerates classes among citizens. In respect of civil rights, all citizens are equal before the law. The humblest is the peer of the most powerful. The law regards man as man, and takes no account of his surroundings or of his color when his civil rights as guaranteed by the supreme law of the land are involved.

Though he was born into a slave-holding Kentucky family, John Marshall Harlan became a key supporter of civil rights for African Americans.

Harlan concluded that the *Plessy v. Ferguson* judgment would in time "prove to be quite as pernicious as the decision made by this tribunal in the Dred Scott Case." That case had declared in 1857 that African Americans were not entitled to the rights of U.S. citizenship.

CHAPTER THREE

THE AGE OF BOOKER T. WASHINGTON

From 1895 until his death in 1915, Booker T. Washington, a former slave who had built Tuskegee Institute (now Tuskegee University) in Alabama into a major center of industrial training for black youths, was the nation's dominant black leader. In a speech made in Atlanta, Georgia, in 1895, Washington called on both blacks and whites to "cast down your bucket where you are." He urged whites to employ the masses of black laborers. Washington felt that excessive stress had been placed on liberal arts education for blacks. He believed that their need to earn a living called instead for training in crafts and trades. In an effort to spur the growth of black business enterprise, Washington also organized the National Negro Business League in 1900. But black businessmen were handicapped by insufficient capital and by the competition of white-owned big businesses.

Washington was highly successful in winning influential white support. He became the most powerful black man in the nation's history up until that time. But his program of vocational training did not meet the changing needs of industry, and the harsh reality of discrimination prevented most of his Tuskegee Institute graduates from using their skills.

BOOKER T. WASHINGTON

Booker Taliaferro Washington was born a slave on April 5, 1856, in Franklin County, Virginia. His mother, Jane Burroughs, was a plantation cook. His father was an unknown white man. As a child, Booker swept yards and brought water to slaves working in the fields. Freed after the American Civil War, he went with his mother to Malden, West Virginia, to join Washington Ferguson, whom she had married during the war.

Booker helped support the family by working in salt and coal mines. He taught himself the alphabet, then studied nights with the teacher of a local school for blacks. When he began attending the school, he had to work five hours each day before class. He called himself Booker Washington until he learned that his mother had named him Booker Taliaferro.

At about age 16 Booker set out for Hampton Normal and Agricultural Institute, which had been

Booker T. Washington was the first African American to have his face on a stamp (which happened in 1940) and on a coin (which happened in 1946).

established by the chief of the Freedmen's Bureau to educate former slaves. He walked much of the way, working to earn the fare to complete the long, dusty journey to Virginia. For his admission test he repeatedly swept and dusted a classroom, and he was able to earn his board by working as a janitor. After graduation three years later he taught in Malden and at Hampton.

A former slave who had become a successful farmer and a white politician in search of the Negro vote in Macon County obtained financial support for a training school for blacks in Tuskegee, Alabama. When

Washington (front row, center left) attracted wealthy and influential sponsors, such as Andrew Carnegie, to the Tuskegee Normal and Industrial Institute.

TUSKEGEE UNIVERSITY

Tuskegee University is an institution of higher learning in Tuskegee, Alabama, about 40 miles (65 kilometers) east of Montgomery. It is the only historically black college or university to be privately controlled yet to have state land-grant status. Tuskegee enrolls a few thousand students, the great majority of whom are African American. The school underwent a series of name changes in its early history and was known as the Tuskegee Institute from 1937 to 1985, when it took its present name.

Booker T. Washington founded the school in 1881 and served as its principal until his death in 1915. He established the school with an emphasis on vocational training, to help African Americans develop economic self-reliance through the mastery of manual trades and agricultural skills. In 1920 Tuskegee's focus shifted to the provision of academic higher education. The renowned agricultural chemist George Washington Carver became head of Tuskegee's agriculture department in 1896. He conducted most of his research at the school. The foundation Carver later created with his life savings still helps to support some of the university's research projects. In conjunction with the U.S. Army Air Corps during World War II, Tuskegee trained the first African American flying unit of the U.S. military, known as the Tuskegee Airmen. The school's third president, Frederick Douglass Patterson (served 1935–53), was the founder of the United Negro College Fund.

the board of commissioners asked the head of Hampton to send a principal for their new school, they had expected the principal to be white. Instead Washington arrived in June 1881. He began classes in July with 30 students in a shanty donated by a black church. Later he borrowed money to buy an abandoned plantation nearby and moved the school there. By the time of his death in Tuskegee in 1915 the institute (now a university) had some 1,500 students, more than 100 well-equipped buildings, and a large faculty.

Washington believed that blacks could promote their constitutional rights by impressing Southern whites with their economic and moral progress. He wanted them to forget about political power and concentrate on their farming skills and learning industrial trades. Brickmaking, mattress making, and wagon building were among the courses Tuskegee offered. Its all-black faculty included the famous agricultural scientist George Washington Carver.

Washington's conciliatory policy appealed to white politicians, many of whom contributed money to Tuskegee. He became an adviser to United States presidents on racial issues and on the appointment of blacks to government positions. Blacks in the South were motivated by his self-help programs, but more militant blacks in the North argued that higher education, rather than vocational training, and political agitation would eventually win full civil rights.

Washington received honorary degrees from Harvard University and Dartmouth College. Among his publications were *Up from Slavery* (1901), his autobiography, and *Frederick Douglass* (1907). Married three times, he outlived his first two wives. He died on Nov. 14, 1915.

Frederick Douglass (1818?–95) was an orator and writer who awakened whites to the evils of slavery and inspired blacks in their struggle for freedom and equality.

GEORGE WASHINGTON CARVER

American agricultural chemist George Washington Carver is one of the best-known figures connected with Booker T. Washington's Tuskegee Institute. Carver helped to modernize the agricultural economy of the South. He developed new products derived from peanuts and soybeans and promoted the planting of these legumes as a way of liberating the South from its dependency on cotton.

George Washington Carver's interest in plants dated back to his childhood, during which his sense for plants earned him the name the Plant Doctor.

Carver was born a slave on a farm near Diamond Grove, Missouri. Although he was freed after the American Civil War he lived until age ten or twelve on his former owner's plantation, where he learned to draw and became interested in plants and animals. He then left and worked at a variety of jobs while he pursued an education. After earning his high school degree he attended Simpson College at Indianola,

Carver would eventually find more than three hundred uses for the peanut alone. This 1938 photo shows him at work in his laboratory.

Iowa, and Iowa State College of Agriculture and Mechanic Arts (now Iowa State University) at Ames. At Iowa he earned a bachelor's degree in agricultural science in 1894 and a master's degree in 1896.

Carver's achievements with plants brought him to the attention of Booker T. Washington. Carver became head of Tuskegee's agriculture department in 1896. In his forty-seven years there the great plant scientist did notable work in scientific agriculture and chemurgy (the industrial use of raw products from plants). He made hundreds of useful products from peanuts and sweet potatoes alone.

Carver was also a painter and a musician. In 1940 he used his life savings to establish the George Washington Carver Foundation for research in agricultural chemistry. Ten years after his death in Tuskegee on Jan. 5, 1943, Carver's birthplace was dedicated as a national monument.

CHAPTER FOUR

VIOLENCE, THE NIAGARA MOVEMENT, AND THE RISE OF THE NAACP

The period of Washington's leadership proved to be one of repeated setbacks for black Americans. More blacks lost the right to vote. Segregation became more deeply entrenched. Anti-black violence increased. However, these dispiriting conditions gave rise to groups that would fight for African American rights.

ANTIBLACK VIOLENCE

Between 1900 and 1914 there were more than one thousand known lynchings. Antiblack riots raged in both the South and the North, the most sensational taking place in Brownsville, Texas (1906); Atlanta (1906); and Springfield, Illinois (1908).

THE BROWNSVILLE AFFAIR

The Brownsville Affair grew out of tensions between whites in Brownsville, Texas, and black infantrymen stationed at nearby Fort Brown. About midnight, on August 13–14, 1906, rifle shots on a street in Brownsville killed one white man and wounded another. White

Among the homes that were fired upon during the Brownsville Affair was that of Louis Cowan, seen to the right in this photo.

LYNCHING

Lynching is a form of violence in which a mob, claiming to administer justice without trial, executes a presumed offender, often after inflicting torture and mutilating the body. The term "lynch law" refers to an unofficial court that imposes a sentence on a person without due process of law. Both terms come from the name of Charles Lynch (1736–96), a Virginia planter and justice of the peace who, during the American Revolution, headed an irregular court formed to punish loyalists, or Americans who supported the British.

Vigilante justice has been practiced in many countries under unsettled conditions whenever informally organized groups have attempted to supplement or replace legal proceedings or to fill the void where institutional justice does not yet exist. Such conditions commonly give rise to acts of genocide. Statistics of reported lynching in the United States indicate that, between 1882 and 1951, 4,730 persons were lynched, of whom 1,293 were white and 3,437 were black. Lynching continued to be associated with U.S. racial unrest during the 1950s and '60s, when civil rights workers and advocates were threatened and in some cases killed by mobs.

commanders at Fort Brown believed all the black soldiers were in their barracks at the time of the shooting; but the city's mayor and other whites asserted that they had seen black soldiers on the street firing indiscriminately, and they produced spent shells from army rifles to support their statements. Despite evidence that the shells had been planted as part of a frame-up, investigators accepted the statements of the mayor and the white citizens.

When the black soldiers insisted that they had no knowledge of the shooting, President Theodore Roosevelt ordered 167 black infantrymen discharged without honor because of their conspiracy of silence. His action caused much resentment among blacks and drew some criticism from whites, but a U.S. Senate committee, which investigated the episode in 1907–08, upheld Roosevelt's action.

THE ATLANTA RACE RIOT

Atlanta, Georgia, had a thriving African American community, but it also had a large population of poor blacks. The 1906 governor's campaign stirred up racial tension, with both candidates debating over how to restrict black voting rights. The local press added fuel to the fire, warning of African American crime and circulating often-false reports of black men sexually assaulting white women.

On the evening of September 22, 1906, a crowd of whites began attacking African Americans and African American–owned businesses in the Five Points neighborhood of the city. The violence continued for several days. At least a dozen people were killed, and many more were deeply shaken by the events.

THE SPRINGFIELD RACE RIOT

The Springfield Race Riot was a brutal two-day assault by several thousand white citizens on the black

Le Petit Journal

Le Petit Journal   **5** Centimes   SUPPLÉMENT ILLUSTRÉ   **5** Centimes   **ABONNEMENTS**

	SIX MOIS	UN AN
SEINE ET SEINE-ET-OISE	2 fr.	3 fr. 50
DÉPARTEMENTS	2 fr.	4 fr. »
ÉTRANGER	2 50	5 fr. »

QUE JOUR—6 PAGES—5 CENTIMES
Administration : 61, rue Lafayette

Le Petit Journal Militaire, Maritime, Colonial..... **10** cent.
Le Petit Journal agricole, 5 cent. ✳ **LA MODE** du Petit Journal, **10** cent.
Le Petit Journal illustré de La Jeunesse..... **10** cent.

e Supplément illustré
CHAQUE SEMAINE **5** CENTIMES

On s'abonne sans frais dans tous les bureaux de poste

Les manuscrits ne sont pas rendus

x-septième année.   **DIMANCHE 7 OCTOBRE 1906**   Numero 829

The Atlanta Race Riot attracted attention from around the world, as this French magazine cover depicting the event illustrates.

community of Springfield, Illinois, in August 1908. Triggered by the transfer of a black prisoner charged with rape (an accusation later withdrawn), the riot was symptomatic of fears of racial equality in the North and the South alike. Almost the entire Illinois state militia was required to quell the frenzy of the mob, which shot innocent people, burned homes, looted stores, and mutilated and lynched two elderly blacks.

Afterward, the population seemed to show no remorse, and some persons even advocated the Southern political strategy of disenfranchisement as

A mob destroyed Harry Loper's restaurant in Springfield, Illinois, after learning that Loper had helped the local sheriff move black prisoners who were accused of crimes against whites to safety.

a means of keeping blacks "in their place." In a moving account of the riot, called "Race War in the North" (Sept. 3, 1908), Southern white journalist William English Walling called for a revival of the abolitionist spirit to stem the tide of such shocking occurrences.

THE NIAGARA MOVEMENT

In 1905 W.E.B. Du Bois, author of *The Souls of Black Folk*, and associates such as William Monroe Trotter, editor of the *Boston Guardian*, organized a conference of African American leaders near Niagara Falls, Ontario. The conference gave birth to the Niagara Movement, whose followers were among the first African Americans to organize against racial discrimination in the United States.

The Niagara Movement developed in response to the continuing oppression faced by blacks in the United States at the start of the 20th century. Despite the progress made since emancipation during the American Civil War, the majority of blacks still did not have the right to vote and also lacked many other civil rights. In addition, many continued to face racial violence; in Georgia alone, 260 blacks were lynched between 1885 and 1906.

In opposition to the idea that blacks could improve their condition through conciliatory policies and accommodation—as advocated by Booker T. Washington—the Niagara Movement sought to end discrimination through direct action. The open controversy over acceptable black leadership dated from 1895, when Washington was invited to address a white audience at the Cotton States and Inter-

Here, a photo of the founding members of the Niagara Movement is superimposed over a photo of Niagara Falls.

national Exposition in Atlanta, Georgia. While emphasizing the importance of economic advancement to blacks, he repeatedly used the paraphrase, "Cast down your bucket where you are." Some blacks were incensed by his comment, "The wisest among my race understand that the agitation of questions of social equality is the extremest folly." Others feared that the enemies of equal rights were encouraged by his promise, "In all things that are purely social we can be as separate as the fingers, yet one as the hand in all things essential to mutual progress."

The Niagara Movement brought together black leaders each year after 1905 in a location associated with antislavery, including Harpers Ferry, West Virginia, and Boston, Massachusetts, but it soon succumbed to internal factions and a lack of funds.

THE NAACP

In 1909 the National Association for the Advancement of Colored People (NAACP), which subsequently took the lead in challenging legal codes unfair to blacks, was established. The group was founded by a group of Niagara members and white liberals following a deadly race riot in Springfield, Illinois, in 1908. Founding members, who initially called themselves the National Negro Committee, included Du Bois, Ida Bell Wells-Barnett, and Mary White Ovington. In 1910 Du Bois founded the new organization's monthly magazine, *The Crisis*, which he also edited until 1934.

The NAACP often has exerted pressure at the national level to combat racial injustice. In 1918

W.E.B. Du Bois helped found the National Association for the Advancement of Colored People and was its outstanding spokesman in the first decades of its existence.

the NAACP helped persuade President Woodrow Wilson to publicly denounce lynching. In 1922 it placed advertisements condemning lynching in major newspapers throughout the United States. The NAACP has also supported civil rights legislation and has itself litigated, through its Legal Defense and Education Fund, cases involving discrimination, including *Brown v. Board of Education of Topeka* (1954), which struck down racial segregation in public schools. The organization has attracted popular support for its positions through programs of education and public information.

CHAPTER FIVE

BLACK LEADERS

Many of the black leaders opposed to Booker T. Washington's approach were involved with the NAACP. W.E.B. Du Bois, William Monroe Trotter, and Ida B. Wells-Barnett were among this dedicated group.

Another voice advocating the advancement of blacks during the period was that of Marcus Garvey, a Jamaican black nationalist who brought his Universal Negro Improvement Association to New York in 1917. The flamboyant Garvey's "back to Africa" movement, based on a doctrine of racial separatism, earned criticism from other black leaders.

W.E.B. DU BOIS

William Edward Burghardt Du Bois was born on Feb. 23, 1868, in Great Barrington, Massachusetts. His parents, Alfred and Mary Burghardt Du Bois, were of African and European ancestry. An excellent student, Du Bois graduated from Fisk University in 1888 and from Harvard College in 1890. He traveled in Europe and studied at the University of Berlin. In 1895 he received a Ph.D. from Harvard. His dissertation, *The Suppression of the African Slave-Trade to the United States of America, 1638–1870*, was published in 1896 as the first volume of the Harvard Historical Studies.

After teaching Greek and Latin at Wilberforce University from 1894 to 1896, Du Bois studied Philadelphia's slums. In *The Philadelphia Negro*, published in 1899, a pioneering sociological study, he hoped to dispel the ignorance of whites about blacks, which he believed was a cause of racial prejudice. Du Bois taught at Atlanta University from 1897 to 1910 and from 1897 until 1914 directed its annual studies of black life.

In *The Souls of Black Folk* (1903), Du Bois declared that "the problem of the Twentieth Century is the problem of the color-line." He criticized the famous black educator Booker T. Washington for accepting racial discrimination and minimizing the value of college training for blacks. Du Bois felt that blacks needed higher education for leadership. In his essay "The Talented Tenth" he wrote, "The Negro race, like all races, is going to be saved by its exceptional men."

The split between Washington and Du Bois reflected a bitter division of opinion among black leaders. In 1905, at Niagara Falls, Canada, Du Bois joined the more militant leaders to demand equal voting rights and educational opportunities for blacks and an end to racial discrimination. But the Niagara Movement declined

Du Bois became the most important black protest leader in the United States during the first half of the twentieth century.

within a few years, and he then helped form another group, which in 1909 became the National Association for the Advancement of Colored People (initially called the National Negro Committee). He edited the NAACP's journal, *The Crisis*, in which he often wrote that blacks should develop farms, industries, and businesses separate from the white economy. NAACP officials, who desired integration, criticized this opinion, and he resigned as editor in 1934. He returned to Atlanta University, and in 1940 he launched *Phylon*, a new magazine about blacks' lives.

Du Bois was interested in African blacks and led several Pan-African congresses. He was awarded the Spingarn medal in 1920 for his efforts to foster black racial solidarity. Although he clashed with Marcus Garvey, the leader of a "back to Africa" movement, and attacked his scheme for an African empire, he lauded Garvey's racial pride.

In his later years Du Bois came to believe that the United States could not solve its racial problems and that the only world power opposed to racial discrimination was the Soviet Union. He was awarded the Communist-sponsored International Peace prize in 1952 and the Soviet Lenin Peace prize in 1958. Du Bois joined the Communist Party of the United States in 1961 and emigrated to Ghana, where he became a citizen, in 1963. He died there on Aug. 27, 1963. He had been married twice, to Nina Gomer and to Shirley Graham, and had two children.

Du Bois was brilliant, proud, and aloof. He once wrote: "My leadership was a leadership of ideas. I never was, nor ever will be, personally popular." Du Bois wrestled with his conflicting desires for both integration and black nationalism. His Pan-African and Communist views

Du Bois wrote several dozen books, including novels, several autobiographies, and nonfiction works on a variety of topics.

removed him from the mainstream of the United States civil rights movement. But he never wavered in his efforts to teach blacks their rights as human beings and pride in their heritage. Among his writings are *Black Reconstruction* (published in 1935) and *Dusk of Dawn* (1940).

IDA B. WELLS-BARNETT

African American journalist and civil rights advocate Ida B. Wells-Barnett led an antilynching crusade in the United States in the 1890s. She used both the newspaper and lectures to get her message across. Wells-Barnett was militant in her demand for justice for African Americans and in her insistence that it was to be won by their own efforts.

Ida Bell Wells was born on July 16, 1862, in Holly Springs, Mississippi, the daughter of slaves. She was educated at Rust University, a freedmen's school in Holly Springs, and at age fourteen began teaching in a country school. After moving to Memphis, Tennessee, in 1884, Wells continued to teach. She also attended Fisk University in Nashville during several summer sessions. In 1887 Tennessee's supreme court ruled against her in a suit she had brought against a railroad that tried to force her to leave a "whites-only" car. A few years later Wells, using the pen name Iola, wrote some newspaper articles that criticized the education that was available to African American children. Her teaching contract was not renewed. She then turned to journalism, buying an interest in the *Memphis Free Speech.*

In 1892, after three friends of hers had been lynched by a mob, Wells began an editorial campaign against lynching. Although her newspaper's

While best known for her antilynching work, Ida B. Wells-Barnett was also involved in other issues. She opposed segregation and supported women's voting rights.

office was sacked, she continued her antilynching crusade, first as a writer for the *New York Age* and then as a lecturer and organizer of antilynching societies. She traveled to many major U.S. cities and twice visited Great Britain to spread her message. In 1895 she married Ferdinand L. Barnett, a Chicago lawyer, editor, and public official, and adopted the name Wells-Barnett. After that she concentrated her efforts in Chicago. She contributed to the *Chicago Conservator*, her husband's newspaper, and published a detailed look at lynching in *A Red Record* (1895). Wells-Barnett also helped organize local African American women in various causes, from the antilynching campaign to the suffrage movement. She founded Chicago's Alpha Suffrage Club, which may have been the first black woman suffrage group.

From 1898 to 1902 Wells-Barnett served as secretary of the National Afro-American Council. In 1910 she founded and became the first president of the Negro Fellowship League, which helped newly arrived migrants from the South. From 1913 to 1916 she worked as a probation officer of the Chicago municipal court. Wells-Barnett died on March 25, 1931, in Chicago, Illinois.

WILLIAM MONROE TROTTER

William Monroe Trotter was an African American journalist and vocal advocate of racial equality in the early 20th century. From the pages of his weekly newspaper, *The Guardian*, he criticized the pragmatism of Booker T. Washington, agitating for civil rights among blacks. Along with W.E.B. Du Bois and others, Trotter helped

state of mind with a feeling of despair
venge. Because their former friends
under the stigma of loving the race, th

seriousl
their en
all but
attitude
white
Negro
due in
measure
ment of
ideals of
whom th
hates.
the polit
the N
many
claimed t
a new da
the South
for the
given W

W. M. TROTTER, a fearless op-
ponent of segregation

William Monroe Trotter's influence was especially strong in his native Boston. Today, the institute for the study of black culture at the University of Massachusetts, Boston, is named after him.

form the Niagara Movement and create the National Association for the Advancement of Colored People (NAACP), from which he later broke ranks.

Raised in the Hyde Park neighborhood of Boston, Trotter graduated with honors from Harvard University as the first black Phi Beta Kappa graduate. After early success in Boston real estate, he founded *The Guardian* in 1901, publishing it in the same building that was once headquarters of the abolitionist newspaper *The Liberator,* published by William Lloyd Garrison. Outspoken in his views, Trotter was arrested for heckling Booker T. Washington in 1903, publicly challenged the policies of Presidents Theodore Roosevelt and Woodrow Wilson, and weighed in on many of the racial conflicts of his time, such as the Brownsville Affair and the Scottsboro case. Trotter also protested a screening of the film *Birth of a Nation.* Over objections by the U.S. government,

THE SCOTTSBORO CASE

The setting for the Scottsboro case was the rural American South in the 1930s, when whites feared racial fraternization as much as blacks feared the mobs that enforced segregation. The defendants in the case were known as the "Scottsboro Boys"—a label that reflected their youth, but even more, in that place and at that time, an epithet used to imply racial inferiority.

During the Great Depression the poor drifted from town to town by stealing rides on freight trains. In a boxcar brawl

(continued on the next page)

(continued from the previous page)

among some hoboes on March 25, 1931, white youths were outnumbered by a group of blacks who threw them off the train. They reported the assault, and a sheriff's posse was alerted to stop the train and arrest the offenders. The nine black youths and two white women found by the posse were taken to the county jail in Scottsboro, Alabama. Armed mobs began to gather after rumors were circulated that the women had been raped. (Some accounts of the case reported that the white hoboes, for revenge, first made up the story of the assault, others that the women framed the blacks because they felt threatened.) Medical reports refuted the women's claims, but the Scottsboro Boys—one only twelve, one disabled, one nearly blind, all illiterate—faced an unsympathetic courtroom. Less than two weeks after their arrest, trials began, lasting only three days. All were convicted, and eight were sentenced to death.

The Communist-affiliated International Labor Defense took the matter to the United States Supreme Court. In a landmark decision *Powell v. Alabama* in October 1932 the convictions were reversed because the defendants had not been adequately represented by counsel in a capital case.

The state of Alabama again tried the defendants. The pattern of retrial, reconviction, and successful appeal continued for several years. By 1937 the opposing attorneys agreed on a compromise: the four youngest defendants would be freed and the others would be paroled within a year. Nevertheless, the last of the Scottsboro nine did not get out of jail until nineteen years after the case began.

he attended the Paris Peace Conference in 1919 as a delegate of the National Equal Rights League.

MARCUS GARVEY

Marcus Moziah Garvey was born in St. Ann's Bay, Jamaica, on August 17, 1887, the youngest of eleven children of Sarah and Marcus Garvey. He attended local schools and at fourteen became a printer's apprentice.

Garvey became devoted to improving conditions for black workers. In 1907 he led a printer's strike in Kingston, Jamaica. Later he toured Central America and South America to organize plantation laborers. In 1912 he went to London, England, where he met blacks from many nations and became fascinated by African history and culture.

Returning to Jamaica in 1914, Garvey established the Universal Negro Improvement and Conservation Association and African Communities League, usually called the Universal Negro Improvement Association (UNIA). Its goals included the promotion of black solidarity, with a special concern for the welfare of African blacks. But the UNIA met apathy from black workers as well as active opposition from the lighter-skinned middle class who did not wish to be identified as blacks. Hoping for support in the United States, Garvey established a branch of the UNIA in New York City in 1917. He taught that blacks would be respected only when they were economically strong, and to that end he founded a newspaper, *Negro World*, as well as other black-owned businesses such as the Black Star Line, a steamship

A fervent black nationalist leader, Marcus Garvey inspired among black people throughout the world a sense of pride in their African heritage.

company. Garvey pledged to establish in Africa a black-governed nation.

With his rallying cry—"Up you mighty race, you can accomplish what you will!"—Garvey attracted thousands of black supporters. He set a passionate example of "a proud black man, honored to be a black man, who would be nothing else in God's creation but a black man." But after 1920 he gradually declined as a popular leader. He was criticized as being a bombastic demagogue or at best a naive dreamer. Garvey-ites were refused permission to settle in the African state of Liberia. The Black Star Line failed from mismanagement, and Garvey was convicted of mail fraud and imprisoned in 1925.

Garvey was released from prison in 1927 but was deported to Jamaica. He worked both there and in London with some success to rekindle interest in the UNIA. A symbol of the determination of blacks to win respect and recognition, he said of himself, "I am only the forerunner of an awakened Africa that shall never go back to sleep."

CONCLUSION

By the first half of the 20th century, crop damage caused many already economically disadvantaged African Americans to leave the Jim Crow South and head for northern cities. Though jobs were not always easy to come by in the North, its cities offered more economic opportunity than the still mostly rural South. African Americans in the North continued to face segregation and discrimination, if not always in the same codified ways they had in the South. In the 1920s, the concentration of talented African Americans in northern cities—in New York in particular—led to the Harlem Renaissance. This flourishing of African American literature, music, and the arts was accompanied by a rise in race consciousness among blacks.

During the 1930s, the Great Depression struck blacks—in the North and South, in cities and in rural areas—hard. However, the New Deal and World

War II brought new job opportunities. Many African American soldiers who had served in the war returned home believing they deserved, and should fight for, equal rights. During the 1940s and 1950s, groups like the NAACP successfully fought to end

These students are doing exercises in front of their segregated school. Segregated schools remained standard throughout much of the United States until the 1950s.

racially restrictive covenants in housing, segregation in interstate transportation, and discrimination in public recreational facilities. In 1954, the Supreme Court finally overturned *Plessy v. Ferguson*, outlawing segregation in schools in *Brown v. Board of Education of Topeka (Kansas).* The civil rights movement worked tirelessly to dismantle what remained of the Jim Crow laws in the 1960s.

TIMELINE

1865

The U.S. Government sets up the Freedmen's Bureau in March to provide practical aid to 4,000,000 newly freed black Americans in their transition from slavery to freedom.

1865

The thirteenth Amendment, which formally ends slavery in the United States, is ratified on December 6.

1866

The Civil Rights Act of 1866 — which declares that all people born in the United States are citizens, regardless of race or "any previous condition of slavery or involuntary servitude" — becomes law on April 9.

1866

The Ku Klux Klan is organized as a social club for Confederate soldiers in Tennessee.

1867

The first buffalo soldiers begin serving in the American West. These African American cavalry regiments would become known for fighting Indians on the frontier.

1868

The fourteenth Amendment is ratified on July 9. It grants citizenship to "all persons born or naturalized in the United States," including former slaves.

1870

The fifteenth Amendment, granting African American men the right to vote, is ratified on February 3.

1870

Tennessee adopts a new constitution on February 23. Among other things, it outlaws intermarriage between African Americans and whites.

1871

Georgia passes the first poll taxes designed to disenfranchise African Americans.

1877

The last federal troops withdraw from the South, bringing the Reconstruction period to an end.

1881

Normal School for Colored Teachers at Tuskegee, known later as

Tuskegee Institute and still later as Tuskegee University, is established in Tuskegee, Alabama.

1882

George Washington Williams's *History of the Negro Race in America from 1619 to 1880* is published.

1887

The Tennessee Supreme Court rules the Chesapeake & Ohio Railroad Company's forceful removal of Ida B. Wells from a whites-only railroad car in 1884 was legal.

1890

Louisiana passes Act 111, also known as the Separate Car Act. It says that railroads operating in Louisiana must provide "equal but separate accommodations" for white and African American passengers.

1892

Anna Julia Cooper's *A Voice From the South* is published. It examines the role of African American women and the struggles they face.

1892

Homer Plessy is arrested on June 7 for challenging Louisiana's Separate Car Act by sitting in a rail car reserved for white passengers.

1895

Booker T. Washington gives his "Atlanta Compromise" speech on September 18, arguing that African Americans should focus on improving their economic well-being instead of fighting for their political rights.

1896

The Supreme Court rules that separate facilities for whites and African Americans are constitutional in *Plessy v. Ferguson* on May 18.

1896

George Washington Carver arrives in Alabama to become the agriculture director of the Tuskegee Institute on October 8.

1897

Alexander Crummell founds the American Negro Academy

to support African American scholarship.

1898

Louisiana passes the first voting law with a grandfather clause.

1899

W.E.B. Du Bois's *The Philadelphia Negro*, a sociological study of the African American population of Philadelphia, Pennsylvania, is published.

1901

William Monroe Trotter founds *The Guardian*, an African American newspaper, in Boston, Massachusetts.

1903

The Souls of Black Folk, by W.E.B. Du Bois, is published. It would become one of the most provocative and influential works of African American literature in the 20th century.

1905

The Niagara Movement holds its first conference, on the Canadian side of Niagara Falls, from July 11 to July 14.

1906

Rifle shots fired during the night of August 13–14 in Brownsville, Texas, set off the Brownsville Affair.

1906

White mobs terrorize blacks in the city of Atlanta, Georgia, from September 22 through September 24.

1908

A race riot breaks out in Springfield, the capital of Illinois, on August 14.

1908

On November 9, the U.S. Supreme Court upholds a Kentucky law forbidding the operation of schools that teach both African American and white students in *Berea College v. Kentucky*.

1909

The National Association for the Advancement of Colored People (NAACP) is founded.

1910

The NAACP publishes the first issue of its monthly magazine, *The Crisis*. At the time, the journal's full title is *The Crisis: A Record of the Darker Races*.

1913

Ida B. Wells-Barnett and Belle Squire found the Alpha Suffrage Club in Chicago, Illinois. It was likely the country's first African American women's suffrage group.

1915

On June 21, the Supreme Court strikes down Oklahoma's grandfather clause in *Guinn v. United States*.

1915

Booker T. Washington dies on November 14. An educator and reformer, Washington was perhaps the most influential African American leader at the time of his death.

1917

Marcus Garvey establishes branch of the Universal Negro Improvement Association in New York City.

GLOSSARY

ADVOCATE A person who argues for or supports a cause or policy.

AGITATE To try to get people to support or oppose something.

APPRENTICE One bound by indenture to serve another for a prescribed period with a view to learning an art or trade.

CONCILIATORY Winning goodwill by being friendly and giving people what they want.

DISCRIMINATION The practice of unfairly treating a person or group of people differently from other people or groups of people.

DISENFRANCHISE To prevent (a person or group of people) from having the right to vote.

EMANCIPATION Being set free from the power of another, particularly being freed from slavery.

ENTRENCHED Solidly established and hard to change.

FRATERNIZATION Spending time with someone in a friendly way, especially when it is considered wrong or improper to do so.

GRANDFATHER CLAUSE A part of a law that says that the law does not apply to certain people and things because of conditions that existed before the law was passed.

JIM CROW LAWS Laws that enforced racial segregation in the South between the 1870s and 1950s.

LYNCHING Putting someone to death (as by hanging) by mob action without legal sanction.

MILITANT Having or showing a desire or willingness to use strong, extreme, and sometimes forceful methods to achieve something.

PRAGMATISM A reasonable and logical way of doing things or of thinking about problems that is based on dealing with specific situations instead of on ideas and theories.

RACIAL SOLIDARITY A feeling of unity between people of the same race.

RECONSTRUCTION The reorganization and reestablishment of the seceded states in the Union after the American Civil War.

SEGREGATION The separation or isolation of a race, class, or ethnic group by enforced or voluntary residence in a restricted area, by barriers to social intercourse, by separate educational facilities, or by other discriminatory means.

SHARECROPPER A farmer, especially in the southern U.S., who raises crops for the owner of a piece of land and is paid a portion of the money from the sale of the crops.

SOCIOLOGY The study of society, social institutions, and social relationships.

SUPREMACY The quality or state of having more power, authority, or status than anyone else.

UNCONSTITUTIONAL Not allowed by the Constitution.

VOCATIONAL TRAINING Education that focuses on skills that will be needed for a particular job.

FOR MORE INFORMATION

Afro-American Historical and Genealogical Society, Inc.

P.O. Box 73067

Washington, DC 20056

(202) 234-5350

Website: http://www.aahgs.org

Founded in 1977, the AAHGS is a national organization with local affiliate chapters in several states. Its promotes historical and genealogical studies of American families, with a particular focus on African American families, who have historically not been well-documented.

The Association for the Study of African American Life and History
Howard Center

2225 Georgia Avenue NW, Suite 331

Washington, DC 20059

(202) 238-5910

Website: http://www.asalh.org

In 1915, Dr. Carter G. Woodson founded ASALH to study and promote the knowledge of black history and culture. In 1926, he established Negro History Week, which evolved into Black History Month in 1976.

Auburn Avenue Research Library

101 Auburn Avenue NE

Atlanta, GA 30303

(404) 730-4001

Website: http://www.afpls.org/aarl

This branch of the Atlanta-Fulton Public Library System is dedicated to the study of African American history and culture. The library has extensive reference and archival collections.

Buffalo Soldiers National Museum

3816 Caroline Street

Houston, TX 77004

(713) 942-8920

Website: http://buffalosoldiermuseum.com

This museum, which opened in 2001, is dedicated to honoring the
African American soldiers who played an important role in the
American West during the late 19th century. Captain Paul J. Mat-
thew, a veteran and military historian, was the museum's founder.

Charles H. Wright Museum of African American History

315 East Warren Avenue

Detroit, MI 48201

(313) 494-5800

Website: http://thewright.org/index.php

In 1998, this museum was renamed for its founder, Dr. Charles Wright.
Wright founded the museum, at the time called the International
Afro-American Museum, in 1965. It aims to educate people about
the African American experience.

The DuSable Museum of African American History

740 East 56th Place

Chicago, IL 60637

(773) 947-0600

Website: http://www.dusablemuseum.org

Founded in 1961, the DuSable Museum seeks to preserve and cele-
brate the contributions of people of African descent. It has a per-
manent collection of over fifteen thousand pieces and also hosts
special exhibitions, workshops, and lectures.

Frederick Douglass National Historic Site

1411 W Street SE

Washington, DC 20020

(202) 426-5961

Website: http://www.nps.gov/frdo

Visitors can tour Cedar Hill, the home that African American leader Frederick Douglass bought in 1877. Douglass, who had been an important abolitionist, continued to be an influential member of the African American community after the Civil War.

George Washington Carver National Monument

5646 Carver Road

Diamond, MO 64840

(417) 325-4151

Website: http://www.nps.gov/gwca

The farm on which George Washington Carver grew up became a national monument in 1943. Visitors can hike along a trail to see the site of Carver's birthplace, a statue of the scientist as a boy, and the 1881 Moses Carver house. Along with guided tours, the park offers nature programs and other activities related to Carver's interests.

Library of Congress

101 Independence Ave SE

Washington, DC 20540

(202) 707-5000

Website: http://www.loc.gov

As the national library of the United States, the Library of Congress houses a vast collection of books, recordings, maps, photographs, and illustrations. This includes a wealth of primary sources for African American history. Selections of its collection have been digitized and are available online as part of the American Memory project's African-American Odyssey presentation.

National Association for the Advancement of Colored People (NAACP)

4805 Mt. Hope Drive

Baltimore, MD 21215

(877) 622-2798

Website: http://www.naacp.org

Founded in 1909, the NAACP has played a central role in advancing the rights of African Americans. It continues to work for social justice today, tackling topics such as media diversity, climate justice, health care, education, and police brutality. The group's website includes biographies of African American leaders, information on legal milestones, and interactive timelines.

North American Black Historical Museum

277 King Street

Amherstburg, ON N9V 2C7

Canada

(519) 736-5433

Website: http://www.blackhistoricalmuseum.org

This museum recounts the story of African Canadians, many of whom were escaped slaves from the United States who fled across the border to freedom. It was founded by members of the Nazrey African Methodist Episcopal Church, which sits next door to the museum.

Tuskegee Institute National Historic Site

1212 West Montgomery Road

Tuskegee Institute, AL 36088

(334) 727-3200

Website: http://www.nps.gov/tuin/index.htm

Visitors to the campus of Tuskegee University can visit several sites that are part of the National Parks Service, including Booker T. Washington's home, the Oaks, and the George Washington Carver Museum.

WEBSITES

Because of the changing nature of Internet links, Rosen Publishing has developed an online list of websites related to the subject of this book. This site is updated regularly. Please use this link to access the list:

http://www.rosenlinks.com/AAE/South

BIBLIOGRAPHY

Alexander, Shawn Leigh. *An Army of Lions: The Civil Rights Struggle Before the NAACP.* Philadelphia, PA: University of Pennsylvania Press, 2013.

Bartoletti, Susan Campbell. *They Called Themselves the K.K.K.: The Birth of an American Terrorist Group.* Boston, MA: HMH Books for Young Readers, 2014.

Collier, Christopher, and James Lincoln Collier. *Reconstruction and the Rise of Jim Crow, 1864–1896.* Amazon Digital Services, 2012.

Dierenfield, Bruce J., and John White. *A History of African-American Leadership* (Studies In Modern History). New York, NY: Routledge, 2012.

Du Bois, W. E. B. *The Souls of Black Folk.* New York, NY: W. W. Norton & Company, 1999.

Gates, Henry Louis, Jr. *Life Upon These Shores: Looking at African American History, 1513–2008.* New York, NY: Knopf, 2010.

Hahn, Steven. *A Nation Under Our Feet: Black Political Struggles in the Rural South from Slavery to the Great Migration.* Cambridge, MA: Bellknap Press, 2005.

Hinman, Bonnie. *Eternal Vigilance: The Story of Ida B. Wells-Barnett.* Greensboro, NC: Morgan Reynolds Publishing, 2010.

Hoffer, Williamjames Hull. *Plessy v. Ferguson: Race and Inequality in Jim Crow America* (Landmark Law Cases and American Society). Lawrence, KS: University Press of Kansas, 2012.

Jones, Angela. *African American Civil Rights: Early Activism and the Niagara Movement.* Santa Barbara, CA: Praeger, 2011.

Labrecque, Ellen. *George Washington Carver* (Science Biographies). North Mankato, MN: Raintree, 2014.

Leckie, William H., and Shirley A. Leckie. *The Buffalo Soldiers: A Narrative of the Black Cavalry in the West.* Revised edition. Norman, OK: University of Oklahoma Press, 2007.

Marable, Manning, and Leith Mullings. *Let Nobody Turn Us Around: An African American Anthology.* 2nd ed. Lanham, MD: Rowman & Littlefield Publishers, 2009.

Medley, Keith Weldon. *We As Freemen: Plessy v. Ferguson.* Gretna, LA: Pelican Publishing, 2012.

Osborne, Linda Barrett. *Miles to Go for Freedom: Segregation and Civil Rights in the Jim Crow Years.* New York, NY: Harry N. Abrams, 2012.

Smith, John David. *We Ask Only for Even-handed Justice: Black Voices from Reconstruction, 1865-1877.* Amherst, MA: University of Massachusetts Press, 2014.

Smock, Raymond W. *Booker T. Washington: Black Leadership in the Age of Jim Crow.* Lanham, MD: Ivan R. Dee, 2010.

Wells, Ida B. *The Light of Truth: Writings of an Anti-Lynching Crusader.* Edited by Mia Bay. New York, NY: Penguin Classics, 2011.

INDEX